PURE FORM

House Design
IVAN RIJAVEC

PURE FORM

House Design
IVAN RIJAVEC

8

EDITED BY STEPHEN CRAFTI

First published in Australia in 2000 by
The Images Publishing Group Pty Ltd
ACN 059 734 431
6 Bastow Place, Mulgrave, Victoria 3170, Australia
Telephone: +(61 3) 9561 5544 Facsimile: +(61 3) 9561 4860
E-mail: books@images.com.au
http://www.imagespublishing.com.au

National Library of Australia Cataloguing-in-Publication Data

Crafti, Stephen.

Ivan Rijavec : pure form.

Bibliography.

Includes index.

ISBN 1 86470 080 7

ISSN 1329 0045

1. Rijavec, Ivan. 2. Architects. 3. Architecture, Modern – 20th
century – Designs and plans. 4. Architecture, Domestic – Designs
and plans. I. Title. (Series : House design ; 8).

720.92

Designed by The Graphic Image Studio Pty Ltd
Mulgrave, Australia

Printed in Hong Kong

CONTENTS

INTRODUCTION

Ivan Rijavec

Ivan Rijavec's architecture stimulates both intellectual and sensory appetites. Intimately physical impressions are formed in the mind as one experiences the unique work of this remarkable Australian architect.

His interests in neurology and the psychology of perception have informed his architecture, however, the conceptual strength and originality of his work is borne from the geometric narrative which he develops from first principles. Rijavec's unique plan graphics have been inspired by abstract expressionist, sexual and baroque allusions. His intentions however, as demonstrated in his architectural forms, argue for a new urban architecture which is both visceral and overtly sensual. His works are difficult to categorise, since they challenge our preconceived notions of what architecture is, even for the initiated.

Professor Phillip Goad, in his book *Melbourne Architecture*, avoids architectural categorisation by referring to the Alessio residence as a 'live in sculpture'. Editor of *Architecture Australia*, Davina Jackson describes Rijavec's work as 'revolutionary in 20th century terms', yet 'tethered to a historical line of anti-Classical expression dating back to the Italian Baroque'. In a subtle way, he tests the perceiver's spatial cognitive capacities, to the point where one becomes self-conscious of the relativity of spatial reality.

Rijavec conceives his work as a continuity of architectural experiences which, he suggests, engage an audience in much the same way as music, dance and cinema. Geometry, 'Ivan's language of invention', is the armature which configures his work. His original use of this language, typified by his preference for irregular, heterotopic geometries, is the key to its understanding. In his words, 'The experience of architecture requires that you move in relation to it, through its volumes and in so doing an architectural score is inscribed in the mind. The score transcends the language of its composition in expressing the essence. When an architecture of subtle geometric complexity is wrought, such that its physical characteristics seem to change relative to the perceiver's movement in and around it, the space becomes alive'.

The development of Rijavec's narrative has been progressive. A vignette which appears in an earlier work may later emerge as the focal idea. His work, characterised by shifts in plane, curvature and direction, creates an intrigue, inviting the audience to participate in unravelling its mysteries. Dynamism consequent of visual tilt, induced as one moves through Rijavec's architecture and the aberrant readings of the same space perceived from different locations, makes this an enduring yet elusive experience which inspires fascination.

In an epoch where rectilinear classicist form has dominated this highly urbanised country, Rijavec's architecture has provided a challenging counterpoint. As this book demonstrates, many already share in Rijavec's vision and delight in the experience of his architecture, the description of which literally challenges the capacities of language.

SELECTED PROJECTS

CHEN RESIDENCE

Kew, Melbourne, Australia
Design/Completion 1998

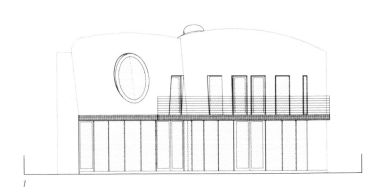

1

The resounding street presence of this home is restrained in comparison to its interior. Two intersecting cones centred in the cubic plane of the facade have been thrust from the sculptural performance within, engaging in a lively debate with its pastiche Victorian and Federation neighbours. On entering the front door, one is captivated by a spectacular volume. Pristine plaster shapes billow like sails into a central void, defying gravity, unfurling outward and upward. This interior, which on first impression seems to have been conceived by a succession of spontaneous gestures, has been wrought from exacting geometries precisely describing changes of incline, plane and curvature. The Baroque geometries of the stair and lantern belie their planimetric genesis in Yin/Yang symbology. Centred in the cube, they have been stretched vertically, beginning with the ribbon-like stair balustrade and culminating in a milk-like swirl forming the lantern. This swirling geometry spirals outward like an explosion of sculptural gestures which have been frozen, erupting exuberantly through the roof and the front and rear facades.

2

The centrifugal performance of this ensemble is testing. Its frozen geometry becomes fluid in the mind's eye, making it clear that its perception is as much a theoretical construction of mind as it is a finite physical reality. It is in this perceptually elusive realisation that its architecture engages with the audience.

The twin balconies overlooking the void on the first floor, which are diagonally opposed and point toward each other, create a subtle tension. Their relationship to the living areas below is theatrical, suggesting an image from Michelangelo's fresco in the Sistine Chapel— 'The Creation of Adam'—where the outstretched fingers of two figures almost touch.

The full-height glass wall separating the open entrance and living areas from the garage includes the automobile's aesthetic in the experience of these volumes. This eccentric brief requirement lends novelty to the interior.

The dominant inverted cone of the street facade conjures images of a pope's mitre, or medieval mask with a visor and nose plate. The form of these references places the windows strategically in relation to street views. The ovular window above and to the right of the entrance serves as a peephole from the Juliet balcony abutting the master bedroom, and the visor frames

landscaped views across the street. The swelling conical curvature of the rear facade is accentuated by a punched-in ovular window. This facade evokes a voluptuous anthropomorphic reading which is distinctively sensual.

Questioned on the neighbours' reaction to the Chen Residence, Ivan replied, 'The erection of the frame and its cladding was an unfolding entertainment, which over the period of its construction must have been persuasive, since the quality of this architecture became discernible to its uninitiated audience, and won them over'.

1&2   North rear elevation
3   Entrance, looking from above
4   Entrance, looking from below

3

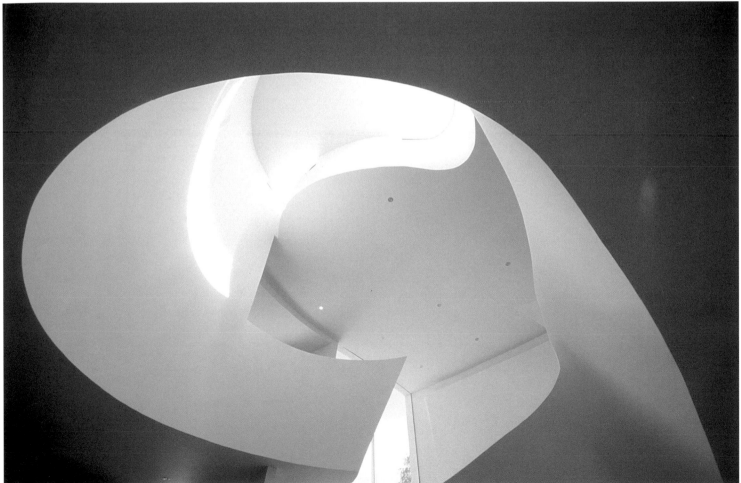

4

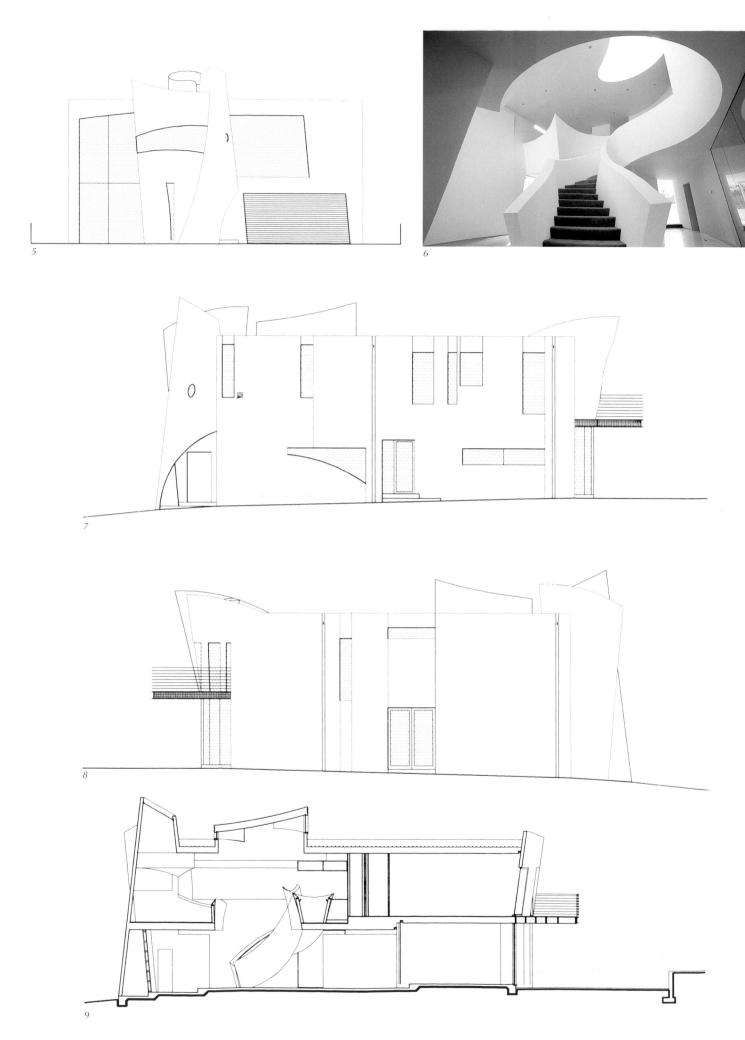

5

6

7

8

9

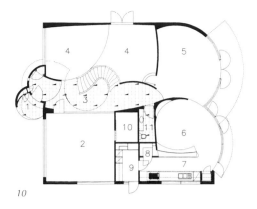

10

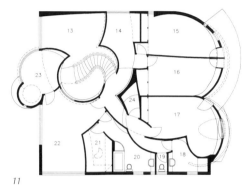

11

1 Entrance
2 Garage
3 Hallway
4 Living
5 Family
6 Meals
7 Kitchen
8 Pantry

9 Laundry
10 Store
11 Powder Room
13 Void (Living below)
14 Study
15 Bedroom
16 Bedroom

17 Guest Bedroom
18 Bathroom
19 WC
20 Ensuite
21 Walk-in Robe
22 Master Bedroom
23 Balcony

5 South elevation
6 Staircase from entrance
7 East elevation
8 West elevation
9 Section
10 Ground floor plan
11 First floor plan
12 Street facade
13 Staircase
14 View from study

12

13

14

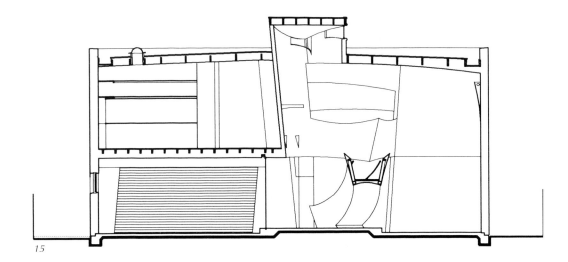

15

16

17

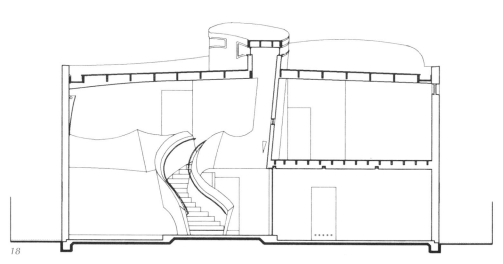

18

19

ALESSIO RESIDENCE

Templestowe, Melbourne, Australia
Design/Completion 1997

1

This striking home is sited on a proscenium-like platform in a valley overlooked by a sea of brick and tiled theme homes. The triangular battleaxe site, located behind dwellings with a street frontage, is flanked on the western edge by a landscaped easement which continues southward to parkland beyond. This idiosyncratic configuration presented an unusual set of opportunities.

Two prow-like forms frame a curtain-glazed wall addressing the private southern vista. On their western face the ship shapes are sliced with vertical and horizontal slots. These windows objectify this Australian suburban spectacle, framing it in sections, like Howard Arkley's paintings.

The brief was driven by the imperative of children yet to be conceived, and for owners Gianna and Massimo Alessio, this meant the living and dormitory areas had to be on one level. This requirement was deftly achieved on a steep site by integrating the primary living floor with a sculpted rear garden. The concrete hull-like form was excavated into the site matching the level of the interior. This enclosed private space, protected from prevailing winds, is an intimate outdoor haven.

'Colour is alive in this home, changing each day and night from one season to the next. The ceiling is punctured with a variety of colour-saturated skylights, truncated moon shapes, tear drops and curvaceous arrows, specifically located and bathing their locale in a halo of tinted light. On a sunny day the citrus yellow tear drops welcome one's arrival, glowing in celebration. They appear to hover a little below the ceiling, casting a spray of yellow on the teal green wall below, blending colour in light. The skylights which are dimmed and illuminated daily by the sun make this house happy', Ivan explains.

The kitchen, with its curved gloss emperite cupboards and granite benchtops, has a nautically profiled island kitchen bench at its geometric focus. Doors leading to the bedrooms and bathrooms are painted in vivid high gloss, combining with the purple, black and white joinery to form abstract colour compositions. The teal blue truncated conical shape of the kitchen's outer side sweeps from the living area to the formal dining areas.

This 'rotunda' is the hub around which the rituals of family life are enacted. Pride of place is given to the most inhabited communal space, the meals area, which enjoys the southern vista toward parkland beyond. 'One of the most wonderful experiences living here, occurs when the fog rolls down the reserve from the south, surrounding us as though the house were an island', explains Gianna. Unusually, the exterior, rendered in red and black super graphics on a white background, emblematises Gianna and Massimo's football team.

2

1 Entry and garage
2 Full-length glazing towards the park
3 Graphic lines
4 A different perspective at night

3

4

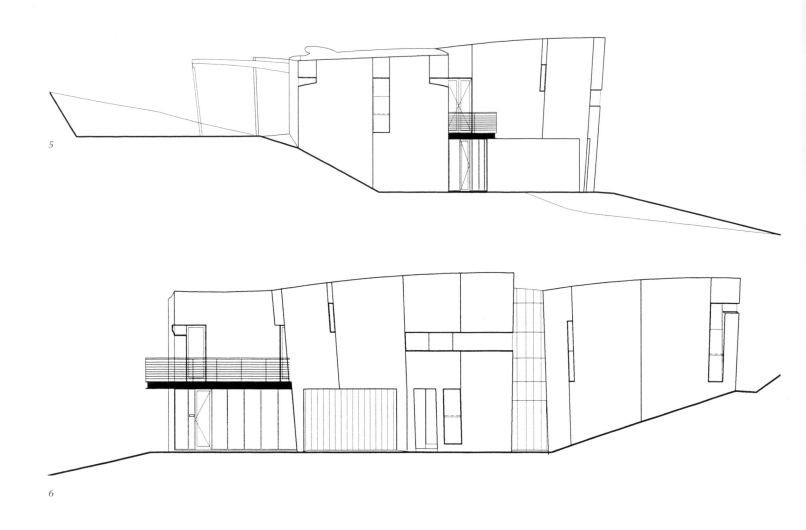

5

6

7

8

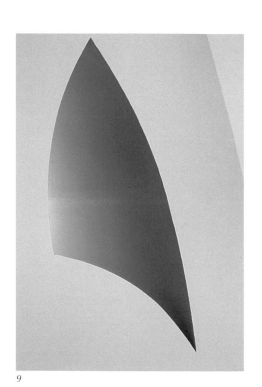

9

10

11

12

13

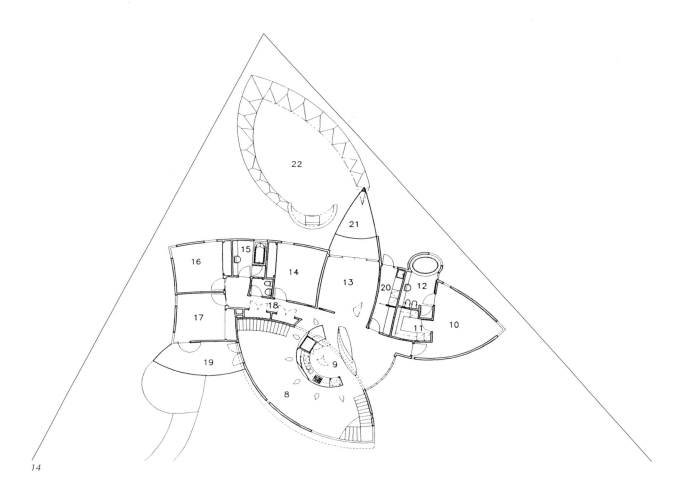

14

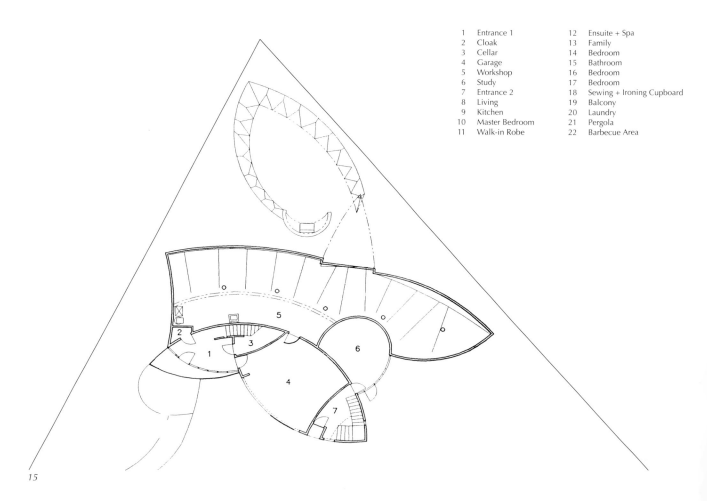

1	Entrance 1	12	Ensuite + Spa
2	Cloak	13	Family
3	Cellar	14	Bedroom
4	Garage	15	Bathroom
5	Workshop	16	Bedroom
6	Study	17	Bedroom
7	Entrance 2	18	Sewing + Ironing Cupboard
8	Living	19	Balcony
9	Kitchen	20	Laundry
10	Master Bedroom	21	Pergola
11	Walk-in Robe	22	Barbecue Area

15

16

17

PENTHOUSE

Central Melbourne, Australia
Design/Completion 1997

This apartment celebrates its aerial location, taking full advantage of the urban geography which it appropriates as a backdrop. From this vantage point the city's topography stretches out between the shafts of Melbourne's skyscrapers. Late in the afternoon reflected light is beamed down from nearby high-rise buildings and this is followed by the dynamic spectacle of the city's nocturnal light show.

For owners Steve Williams and Vicki Battin, commuting to the city everyday had become a chore. Steve's brief was simple: 'Three words in fact. Space, light and air that translated into volume', says Ivan. 'Though we are embedded in a dense urban location,' Vicki explains, 'We feel like we're in the open, miles from anywhere yet in the thick of it, three minutes walk to work'.

The interior is completed in a rich colour palette which includes deep purple, blue and vivid green high-gloss doors, set against the rich hue of the new polished Jarrah and existing Baltic pine floors. Upon entering, one approaches the fuchsia arch en route to the floor above and a large conical skylight rendered in cobalt blue dominates the procession to the first floor.

Bedrooms and a spacious library are located on the lower level, and open living areas served by decks to the north and south are located on the upper floor. The arched window which figures prominently in the heritage-listed street facade is celebrated within by an augmentative construction devised to overcome an awkward junction with the new floor level. The staircase angling up through the void to the upper floor is reminiscent of a gangplank, suggesting one is boarding a craft as one ascends to the living areas.

To create the volume Steve and Vicki had briefed, Rijavec conceived a gull wing roof, formed in aluminium, which cranks in an elliptical trajectory from the higher eastern parapet across to the lower western edge of the building. Internally the ceiling form billows down in three convex folds from a height of approximately six metres to floor level.

A complexity of scale within affected by the cascading ceiling meeting the floor, creates an intimate and reassuring ambience on the western side. By contrast the cathedral-like volume on the eastern side inspires awe as it ascends through the skylight. From this volume, having negotiated a compressed space in the airlock, one is struck by the strip of mirrors which circumscribe the powder room at eye level—they ricochet infinite reflections and the surprise is immense.

1   Front elevation
2   View from the street
3   Rear elevation upper floor
4   Living room
5   Northern rooftop terrace
6   Canopy over northern terrace

1

2

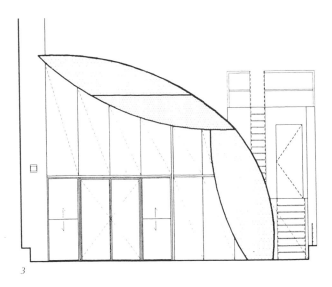

3

4

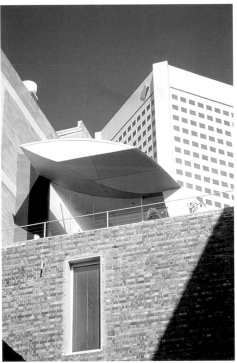

5

6

7

7 View from below
8 Upper level floor plan
9&10 First floor open plan living area
11 Section
12 West elevation
13 Living area
14 View from the terrace

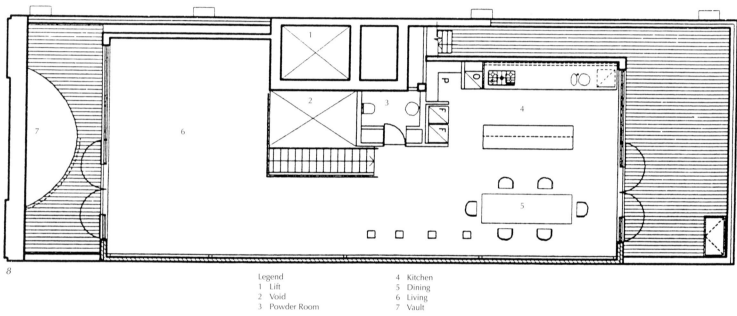

8

Legend
1 Lift
2 Void
3 Powder Room
4 Kitchen
5 Dining
6 Living
7 Vault

9

10

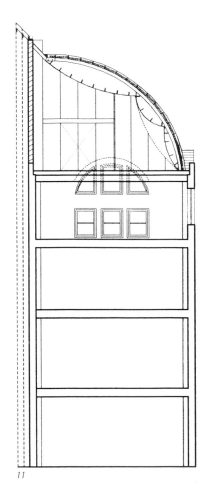

11

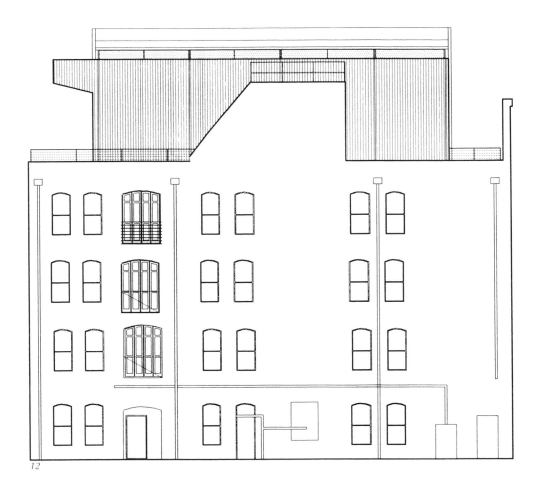

12

13

14

FREELAND RESIDENCE

Fitzroy, Melbourne, Australia
Design/Completion 1994

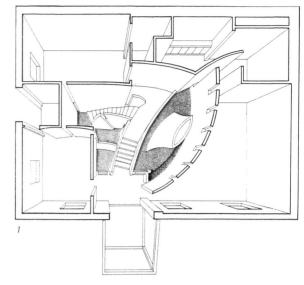

1

This warehouse conversion is the second in a trio of works which configure a curvilinear geometry within a cubic shell. The first, completed immediately upon graduation, slots two sculpted ensuites into the cubic form of a Georgian terrace. The Freeland residence, finished nine years later, expands on this by implicating the whole interior in the sculptural strategy. Four years subsequently the external cubic shell of the Chen residence was conceived to create a related formal dialogue between the new orthogonal exterior and the sculptural interior, which in this case projects outside the cube.

The Freeland interior takes even design aficionados by surprise. A sophisticated composition of curvaceous volumes and subtly twisting forms creates a naturally lit internal realm around which the living, dining and dormitory areas are located. 'This geometry, set in the orthogonal definition of the warehouse shell, converges in a three-dimensional vortex where the subtly twisting fireplace diminishes as it rises through the space, drawing one's gaze to the cluster of skylights in the ceiling above', Rijavec explains. The adjacent enclosed spaces are naturally illuminated by slot windows which articulate the converging elements and allow light penetration from the void and from one space to another.

The kitchen, articulated in an abstract graphic pattern of greens, greys and black laminates, is an intimate space which by contrast accentuates the scale of the central void. This is a space in which Ivan's cinematic analogies are entirely persuasive in describing the architectural experience. In negotiating its volumes, one is conscious of moving from one scene to another in a seamless procession that offers new vistas and perspectives, with each turn and rebound. As one moves around this space, perceptions from different vantage points in and around it read quite differently, engendering the magnification of one's sense of volume, such that it seems vast.

The bleak industrial exterior of this structure belies the sculptural magic within which, for those fortunate enough to enter, unravels like a film into one of the best cinematic events in this part of town.

2

4

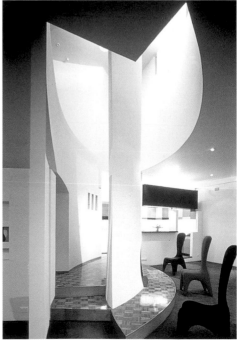

5

3

6

7

8

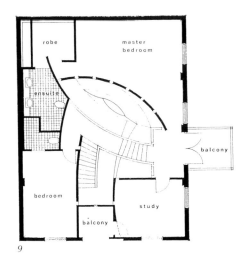

9

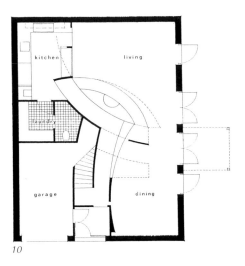

10

11

12

BARTHOLOMEW APARTMENT

Central Melbourne, Australia
Design/Completion 1997

1

2

Rijavec's conception for this micro volume was a super-geometric order that perceptually expands the volume well beyond its actual physical dimensions. In this space, one is charmed by the simultaneous realisation of its felt intimacy and perceived immensity. This simple, yet complex, space was created in the sweep of one brushstroke, which cuts a swathe across the living areas integrating them into one expansive, yet intensely intimate volume.

Full-height milled steel which lines the lobby entrance wall accentuates the surprise awaiting within. Having crossed this threshold, the apartment literally draws you into a realm of subtle complexity. The sculptured alcoves lining the main living room wall push out horizontally in counterpoint to the embrace of its curvature. An elliptically arched and mirrored alcove that serves as a bar reads as a portal to a (nonexistent) space beyond. The vastness of this space is subconsciously realised in the perception of its elongations, expansions and compressions—all conveyed with consummate ease.

The circular kitchen is 'a warm nut-like space', according to Ivan. Mahogany veneered cupboards enrich this anthropomorphic capsule, where everything is within arms-reach—it is a single person's dream come true. Within the bedroom, concealed from the main living areas by the tilting edge of this apartment's canted wall, one's senses are recharged by the richness of ruby lacquered full-height robe doors. From this space a steel grey door leads to a beautifully proportioned white cube which accommodates a minimalist ensuite reflected infinitely in the mirror at its end.

This rare space has a presence which seems audible, it hums with mystery and intelligence.

1,3&4
 Living room
2 View towards bedroom
5 Bedroom

3

4

5

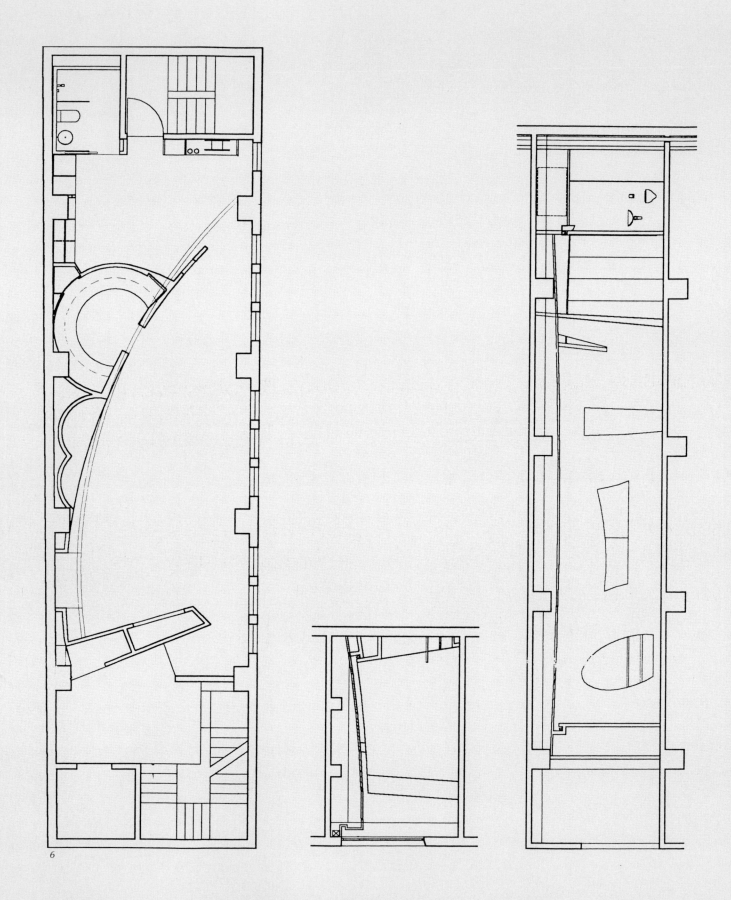

6

7

8

9

10

11

12

RIJAVEC ARCHITECTS' OFFICE/PRIVATE APARTMENT

Fitzroy, Melbourne, Australia
Design/Completion 1986

1

Rijavec's warehouse was a benchmark of its time, fuelling the blaze of conversions in the area. *Interior Design's* editor in 1987, Herbert Ypma, described it as follows: 'Deep in the heart of Fitzroy is a space, a beautiful space; a kill for, sell your mother for space'.

The warehouse comprises Rijavec Architects' office, a library, conference area and a private apartment. Constructed in 1901 by a suffragette, the building originally served as a hat factory. Since then it has had a number of industrial incarnations, the most recent being as a shoe factory.

Rijavec Architects on the ground floor is in an open-plan configuration and is screened from the main entrance by a curved wall punctuated with a vertical slot. The slot is on axis with internal columns and provides a discreet view to the office beyond. Edwardian stairs in the entrance areas at the front and rear are the only remnants of the original interior.

The first floor is configured as a number of discreet zones interconnected in a subtly dynamic space enclosed by two large arcs of variable curvature. These arcs extend to the underside of enlarged trusses wrapped in plaster casts, which lends them a sculptural quality. Flanking the trusses, two overlapping bulkheads make the transition to the orthogonal geometry of the pitched roof above. Trios of deeply recessed clerestory windows, which borrow light from the adjacent enclosed spaces, punctuate the bulkheads lending a celestial ambience.

By contrast, the kitchen is a riot of primary colour arranged in *de stijl* composition, which is repeated in the tiles and laminates of the bathroom. Vibrant reds, yellows, vivid white and striking blue laminates articulate the joinery which provides a lively constructivist interlude in an otherwise pristine interior. Externally the only visible evidence of change is a projecting steel balcony, which heralds the geometry of a remodelled interior.

2

3

4

5

1&4   Dining area
2   Street facade
3   Rear facade
5   Living areas

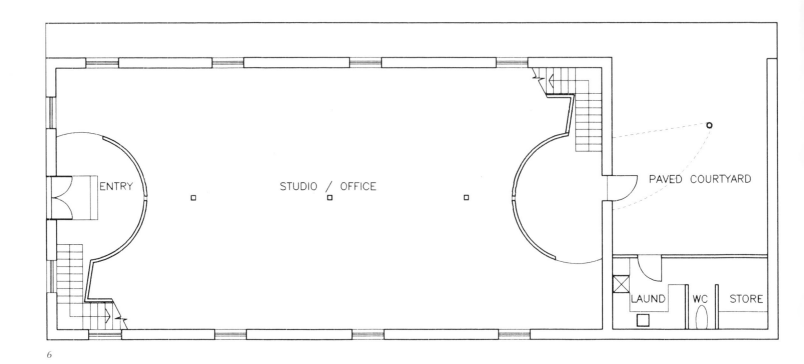

6

6 Ground floor plan
7 Kitchen
8 First floor plan
9&10 Dining area

7

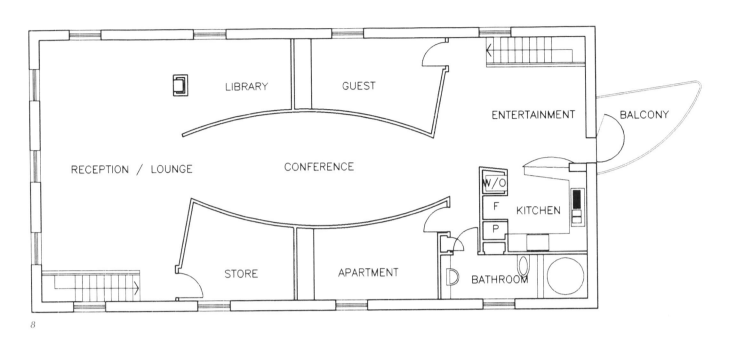

8

9

10

LARA SHOE FACTORY/ STUDIO APARTMENTS

Fitzroy, Melbourne, Australia
Design/Completion 1989

An uncertain genesis spawned a curious brief for this project. The client, Carol Droomer, purchased this large warehouse with the intention of establishing a gallery. A partnership being formed to operate the enterprise dissolved in the schematic phase of the design and a speculative development proposing the 300 square metre shell be divided in two was initiated. It was clear the subdivided spaces would appeal to a variety of end-users and Carol wanted to maximise the market potential of the two allotments by proposing several alternative functions, including, residential accommodation, studio space and exhibition areas.

Flexibility was achieved by incorporating fully glazed courtyards centred on one side of a predominantly open-plan configuration. The structural window mullions run full height and are spaced at half-metre intervals so as to achieve a smooth curvature to the inner wall. The diaphanous views across the open plan of the ground floor and through the courtyards lend these volumes an expansive atmosphere. Ironically two small courtyards constituting only 20 square metres in plan achieve this ambience. These micro landscapes are configured within the plan geometry, which achieves efficient circulation and separation between functional areas, without need for doors and corridors.

The kitchen of the southern most allotment, decorated in a variety of green laminates, nestles under an emerald bulkhead which projects just over the elevated bar facing the dining room. The raised ceiling of the adjacent thoroughfare is painted in a deep burgundy. This vibrant colour palette is subdued by a soft leaf green, which describes the outer perimeter of the shells. Accents in black, yellow, bright blue and orange lighten one's spirit in these airy spaces.

Interior space dissolves into and through the gardens, such that every internal space appropriates a view. 'Standing in the garden you get a doll's house impression of each apartment,

yet from within, each space is visually secure', explains Ivan. To the occupants the interior has a refreshing green heart, a welcome relief from the urban surroundings. Movement on the stairs is sensed in spaces above and beyond the warehouses which take on a theatrical character, paradoxically giving them the appearance of the gallery originally envisaged by Carol.

1

2

3

1 View from first floor deck
2 View from courtyard
3 Living area
4 Graphic staircase
5 A sense of transparency

4

5

6&10   Floor plan
   7   Staircase
   8   First floor living area
   9   Ceiling detail

6

7

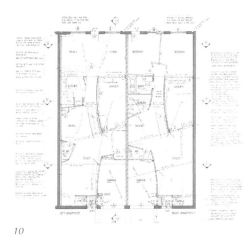

10

8

9

11

12

13

11 First floor
12 Kitchen/dining area
13 A sense of transparency

MANIFOLD RESIDENCE

Brunswick, Melbourne, Australia
Design/Completion 1989

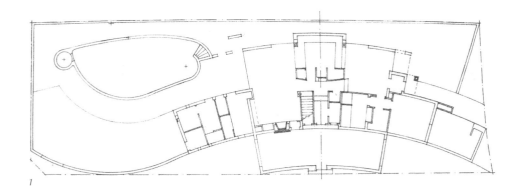

The unique presence of this house is largely due to its implied ownership of the adjacent public laneway. This phenomenon, rare in residential contexts, comes about as a result of the unusual relationship the house assumes in relation to the lane. Its subtly curving monolithic form stretches out to the street by way of a wall which steps down to form the front fence, thus appropriating the space outside its boundaries in the same way that large public buildings imply ownership over their adjacent spaces.

'The client wanted to be able to enter the centre of the house from the garage and this was achieved by sliding it to the desired location along the southern arc of the house. There is no reason why additional rooms couldn't be added, extending this geometric armature toward the rear of the house without compromising its form', explains Ivan.

Windows to the street are carefully framed around selective views and integrated in the cubic composition of the front facade. Each of the primary elements in the composition was to be rendered in a different colour. Recessed slots were to have articulated changes in colour, thereby breaking down this monolith into an animated abstract relief.

The property crash of 1989 to 1991 saw to it that the house remained unfinished for several years, 'appropriately taking on the appearance of a 20th century ruin', says Ivan. Brunswick, now a thriving inner city suburb and home to the *avant-garde*, was a depressed area a decade ago when construction of the Manifold residence was paused. Its bold form was then an anomaly to the despondent spirit of the area.

1   Floor plan
2   Street facade
3   Selecting the views

3

4

5

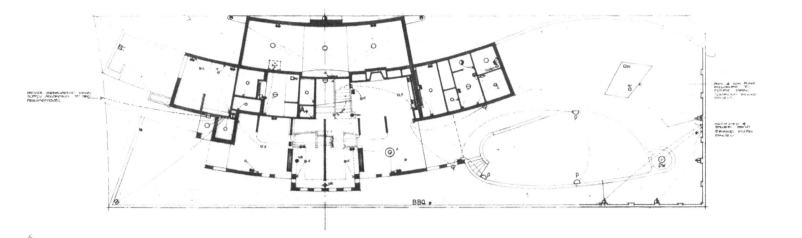

6

7

4   A sense of protection
5&7   Street facade
6   Floor plan

FOARD WAREHOUSE

Windsor, Melbourne, Australia
Design/Completion 1990

Wendy Foard, the inspired client for this project, was a budding young artist when the design was commissioned in 1989. Her brief was to separate the building into four distinct areas; two self-contained studios on the ground floor which would be leased out, and a private apartment and studio for Wendy on the floor above.

Rijavec's solution preserved the clear span of the existing structure by incorporating geometrically distinct fragments along the two party walls on the upper floor. The central space, formed between a curvilinear geometric ensemble on one side and an angular one on the opposite side, has a micro urban scale. Between these two forms the space is cradled in much the same way as buildings frame a street. 'Standing in the middle of the room, it's like being outside, with buildings on either side. The living/dining area conjures the ambience of a laneway, and sitting at the dining table one can imagine being at a table on the pavement outside one's favourite restaurant', explains Ivan.

This formation creates a sense of escape for Wendy, a relief from the intensity of her work. The kitchen, sheltered under a canopy projecting from the angular ensemble into the dining area, has all the appearances of a street kiosk. Bright green, grey, silver and black accented laminates transform the area into an abstract muse.

A new full-length lantern surmounting the existing trusses provides ideal natural lighting conditions, and a stair flanking the curvilinear bedroom wing accesses a north-facing deck with vistas down Chapel Street towards the city centre. From this vantage point, looking back through the array of trusses, one is immediately struck by the grandeur of this space.

1

The front and rear facades were substantially remodelled and rendered in colour. Against these backdrops, vibrant hues emerge through the windows, signalling Ivan's vivid interior and its artist in residence.

3

2

1   Street facade
2   Trusses and staircase lines
3   Kitchen

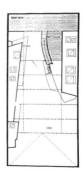

FIRST FLOOR

MEZZANINE (FIRST)

4

4   Floor plan
5,6&7
    Staircases
8   Kitchen

5

6

7

8

WELLINGTON STREET RESIDENCE

Clifton Hill, Melbourne, Australia
Design/Completion 1989–1990

The primacy of colour and form in this design has been infused with 'Reebok bounce and espresso concentration', according to Ivan, which at first captivates and then energises. Melbourne architect Hamish Lyon described the space as follows: 'The large open volume at the rear provides the clearest demonstration of the architect's intention. Set against the parallel boundary walls a super-scaled vivid yellow wall arcs its way through dining and family areas, establishing a new order. This primary stroke is both formal and functional since, within its form, the utility of the bath, laundry, kitchen and powder rooms are discreetly contained, allowing an uninterrupted flow of space through adjoining areas. The baroque lines of the kitchen bench act as a pivot between the relative security provided by the sweeping bulkhead over, and the larger scaled volume of the living area adjacent'.

The kitchen abstracts which typify Ivan's early work, reach a crescendo in this project where pink, black, yellow, vivid green, red and metallic silver are resonantly juxtaposed. In this lively environment, each of the elements is shuffled loosely together, like a child's interlocking puzzle, almost solved but left just short.

Rijavec celebrates the power of colour in dislocating architectural form such that fresh elements appear to invade the space with the optimistic vibrancy of a new order. The interior has been completed with brightly coloured furniture integral to the space.

1

2

1 Entry
2 Kitchen
3 Living area

3

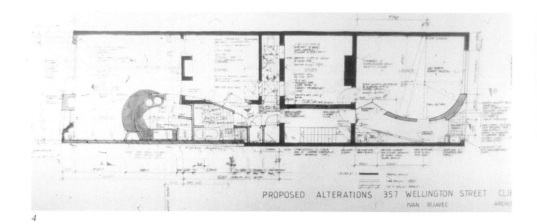

PROPOSED ALTERATIONS 357 WELLINGTON STREET CLI...
IVAN RIJAVEC ARCHI...

4

4   Floor plan
5   Kitchen sinks
6   Living area
7   Kitchen

5

6

7

CONDOMINIUM TOWERS

St Thomas Walk, Singapore
Design 1994–1995
Project shelved

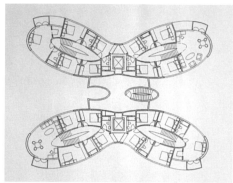

1

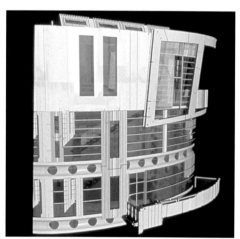

2

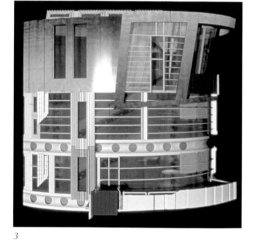

3

The St Thomas Walk project, comprising three condominium towers ranging from twenty five to thirty storeys, was commissioned for a site ten minutes from Singapore's retail precinct in Orchard Road.

'The improbability of the plan graphic, which can be likened to a flower, four-leafed clover, a propeller or back to back peanuts, has been the focus of comment on this project. Ironically this design outcome belies the generative prototype from which the form was derived', Rijavec explains.

The design was developed from the 'H' plan prototype, a four apartment per floor tower, by substituting the four rectilinear apartment cells with five intersecting ellipses and by mirroring the plan and rotating the apartment cells around the core. 'This operation serves to both eliminate the back of the house condition and to position each of the apartment cells such that unobstructed views are maintained around the outer periphery of the ellipse. A generosity of aspect can therefore be achieved in the site plan such that each of the petals appropriate diagonal views between the towers', clarifies Ivan.

Each petal is similarly shaped but of a different size and layout, ranging from one to three stories and two to four bedrooms. The living rooms are given primacy of place in the outer foci of the ellipses. Here, in the ambience of a scaled up cockpit, panoramic views would be enjoyed.

Both precast masonry and aluminium-clad designs were prepared and presented to the client who resolved to shelve the project in favour of other developments planned for Indonesia.

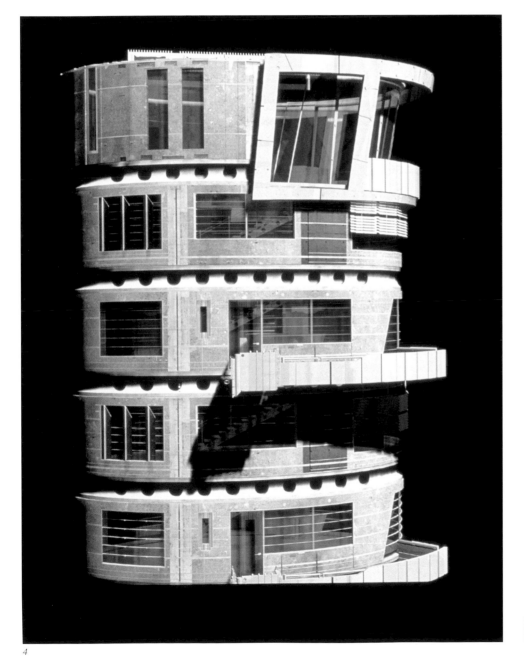

4

5

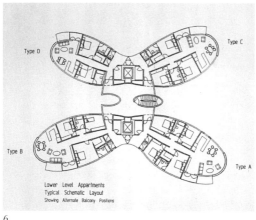

Type D

Type C

Type B

Type A

Lower Level Appartments
Typical Schematic Layout
Showing Alternate Balcony Positions

6

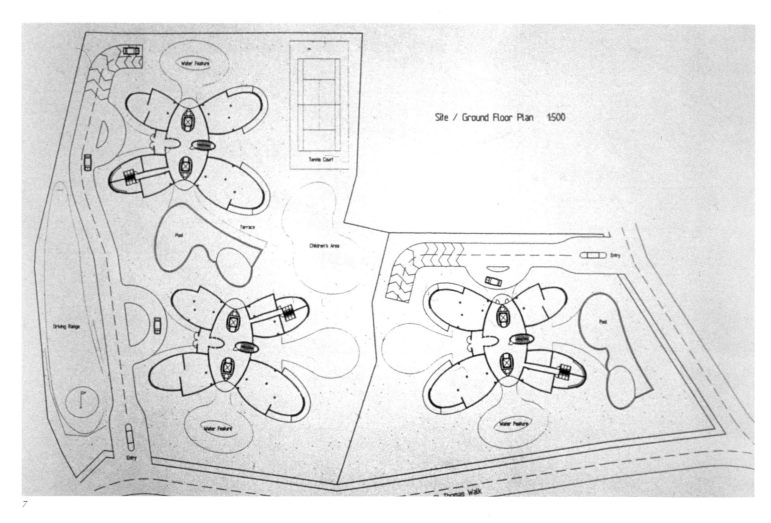

Site / Ground Floor Plan   1:500

Water Feature

Tennis Court

Pool

Terrace

Children's Area

Driving Range

Water Feature

Entry

Entry

Pool

Water Feature

Thomas Walk

7

6   Floor plan
7   Site plan
8–10   Computer images

8

9

10

BLISS BAR

Armadale, Melbourne, Australia
Design/Completion 1992–1994

The bar, fabricated in one seamless sheet of stainless steel, is formed by a geometric transition between two different sized inverted cones. Fabricated off-site, it was installed in one piece by removing two stainless steel disks on the counter and fixing it to the floor with two elongated steel bolts.

This enigmatic object arouses a host of abstract associations which reinforce the enduring romance we have with auto engineering. A high gloss black stone floor reflects its form and those of the matching bar stools. Two conical tables located away from the bar wrap around existing columns disguising their presence.

1

2

1   Stainless steel bar and stools
2   Bar and stools
3   Energising the interior

3

FOUR LEAF CLOVER

Flinders Lane, Melbourne, Australia
Design/Completion 1992–1994

The project had its ideological genesis in the geometry of the St Thomas Walk development and was to accommodate four penthouses surmounting a heritage structure. These tapering forms were calculated so as to reduce the superstructure's impact from street level.

In this case the elliptical geometry was stretched across the L-shaped platform of the existing roof structure so as to create residual outdoor spaces accommodating paved decks and lap pools. Each of the conical ellipses was to accommodate a three-storey penthouse. The ambitious brief for this project survived the rigors of three local authority design panels and a town planning permit was eventually granted, however the vision remains unrealised.

Top left: View from above
Middle: Detail
Bottom left: View from southeast
Right: View from east

ARMADALE CINEMA

Armadale, Melbourne, Australia
Design 1993–1994

This project began as a joint venture between the local council and a film distributor and was intended to resurrect an inner suburban shopping precinct in decline. A tortuous planning process took the best part of a year to negotiate, including an extended period at the Appeals Tribunal. A corporate cinema conglomerate bought the project and resold it, placing a caveat on the contract of sale preventing its development as a cinema so as to increase the profitability of their nearby Cineplex.

The project included two restaurants, substantial rear car parking, and a seven-screen cinema. The auditoria were graded in size from three hundred seats down to fifty, so that a popular film could be gradually phased out as its audience diminished.

The facade was conceived in two parts comprising a recessed superstructure which floats above the second floor car parking level, and a system of complex curving planes on the ground and first floors. The sculptural collage of super-scaled theatrical masks constructed from stainless steel, black chrome and sealed brass addresses the mobile street audience directly.

Part of the recessed superstructure constituted a screen for night projection and the gloss metallic exterior of the substructure was to be illuminated. This projected visual entertainment recalls the heyday of film in the 1930s when cinema architecture reflected the excitement of a vibrant new art form. S. Charles Lees aphorism, 'The show begins on the sidewalk', applies here.

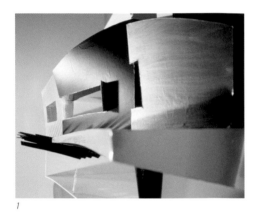

1

2

3

4

1&2 Street facade
3&4 Model
5 Street facade looking up from pavement

5

SUTANTO HIGH-RISE PALACE

Djarkarta, Indonesia
Design 1994

1

2

3

Adjunct professor, Melbourne architect and author Norman Day states: 'This house for an Indonesian banker is pure farce, shafts of concrete plates, each containing a different functional purpose, slice through space joined only at the core...This is pure whimsy...The design captures the spirit of Zaha Hadid and blows it out of the water by being believable. This is a hallucination that could be real. The house will not be built and actually never was to be, but such a test of nerve by an architect measures the skills, hones the designs, maybe provokes the self to dig deeper, peel more off the fruit, squint harder at the sun'.

4

5

1   Digital collage
2–5   Sketches

BATHROOM *TRANSPLANT*

Fitzroy, Melbourne, Australia
Design/Completion 1979

This project, referred to as a transplant since it replaces the building's services with a form reminiscent of the human heart, was Rijavec's first postgraduate commission. It reflects ideas developed in his final year thesis and is the ideological genesis of the Chen and Freeland designs which emerged nearly two decades later.

A plug-in sculpture resolves two ensuites enlarged to accommodate spa baths in the limited area available on the first floor of a Georgian Terrace. The concept includes catering and entertainment functions on the lower floor, for use by Sydney advertising executives visiting their Melbourne office. The sumptuous ensuites and master bedrooms, complete with entertainment systems integrated in the sculptural walls, reinforce the prevailing myths of life in the fast lane of corporate advertising.

6

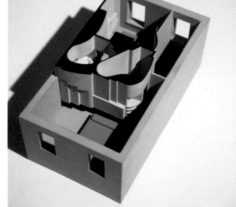

6&7   Three-dimensional model

7

VIEWING ROOM

The Gallery of Western Australia's State Collection, Perth, Australia
Design/Completion 1986

1

2

Ivan had been contracting to a large practice on the design of Melbourne's morgue where he was struck by the soulless anonymity of a space called the viewing room. It was no larger than a disabled toilet and had a curtained window at one end providing visual access to the deceased. Relatives were led to this room and, at the appropriate moment, the curtain was drawn revealing the body. Morgue attendants referred to this emotionally searing time as 'the moment of realisation' which was often followed by wrenching scenarios.

Rijavec, whose father had recently died, was numbed by the depersonalisation of death in this context which had turned it into a kind of peep show. He conceived the ten-millimetre plate steel model in answer to this. The *maquette*, laced with the symbolism of funerary architecture, has a strange presence which prepares one's sensibilities for 'the moment of realisation'.

3

1–3   Maquette

NOISE WALLS AND SOUND ATTENUATING STRUCTURE

Melbourne, Australia
Design 1995

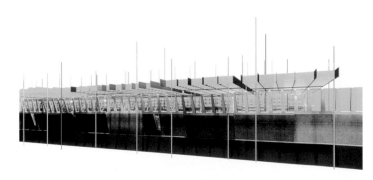

1

The three competition proposals which follow provide insights into Rijavec's conceptual dexterity. They are a departure from the sculptural style for which he is predominantly known, indicating the broad theoretical basis of his work.

This proposal, submitted for the first stage of Melbourne's South Eastern Freeway limited design competition, included noise wall, bridge and sound attenuating structure designs. Noise wall reliefs made of metal and masonry were designed to be cast into concrete walls. Their rhythmic placement was conceived as a travelscape which, when viewed at 100 kilometres per hour, unfolded in a narrative addressing the identity of the locales through which the freeway passed. A sound attenuating structure comprising perforated baffles of different colours, supported on a forest of slender columns, was designed to attenuate noise projected upward from a valley to residential areas situated on the surrounding hillsides.

Rijavec's interests in perceptual psychology and the structure of music is evidenced in these designs. The score inscribed in the walls becomes audible at freeway speed unfolding as a series of compressions, elongations and punctuations, intended as a relief for commuter boredom.

2

1   Sound attenuating structure viewed from
    the landscaped area adjacent
2   Detail
3   Digital collage of sound walls

3

MUSEUM COMPETITION

Melbourne, Australia
Design 1995

1

2

Rijavec integrates the museum with the Exhibition Gardens, creating civic spaces which enable access over and through the museum structure without breach of security. In these spaces, piazzas telescope down into museum courtyards connecting the everyday café and promenade activities above with the retrospective intensity of history below.

'We sought to supercharge the exhibition building's architecture by dovetailing its northern transept into an abstracted piazza contained by the museum's flanking wings', explains Ivan. The relationship between the exhibition building and the new museum alludes to the Piazza Di San Pietro, which aggrandises St Peter's Basilica in Rome and provides a fluid integration with its surrounding urbanscape. Similarly, the northern transept of the exhibition building provides a monumental focus, charging the square it fronts with a resonant sense of place.

3

Digital collages:
1   Detail of entrance
2   View from southwest
3   Bird's-eye view

CIRCULAR QUAY

Sydney, Australia
Design 1997–1998

Rijavec's concept choreographs the spectacle of urban congestion into an expression of metropolitan vitality where commuters, parading citizens and tourists negotiating this three-dimensional matrix simultaneously become part of the spectacle and voyeurs of its theatre. Piers, which moor Sydney ferries, take the form of an unwound starfish. Above this, 'biomorphed' concourses punctuated by irregular conical lightwells reinforce the new wavy shoreline, where the city meets the harbour.

A metaphoric form which dominates the ensemble seems like a gigantic bat or manta ray and is the key to the tripartite connection between the Quay, the Sydney Harbour Bridge and the Opera House. This audacious design is both powerful and challenging in the context of Sydney's international landmarks.

1

Digital collages:
1   *View from city*
2   *View along expressway*
3   *View from above*

2

3

FIRM PROFILE

Ivan Rijavec
B Arch RMIT 1979, M Arch RMIT 1992, RAIA

Principal, Rijavec Architects

Ivan Rijavec commenced his architectural education at Curtain University, Perth in 1969 and after completing the lower tier course, was granted a bursary to study in Europe. The purpose of the study was to trace the development of Western Civilisation through Greece, Central and Western Europe. On completion of the term of the scholarship, Ivan remained abroad for five years, studying and working in London and Sweden.

Rijavec returned to Australia in 1977, completing his first degree at the Royal Melbourne Institute of Technology in 1979. Prior to devoting himself full-time to his own practice, he was contracted to some of Melbourne's major firms and the Public Works Department as a designer on specific projects where design quality was deemed a priority. In his capacity of associate director at Bates Smart, Ivan assumed senior design roles on major projects. During this period Ivan gleaned a thorough grounding in the design and documentation of major urban projects.

Rijavec Architects was established in January 1979 and since then has practised in most conventional areas of architectural practice. It is known for innovative contemporary work which expresses relevant cultural idioms of today.

The practice has been recognised by the architectural profession, architectural media and by academic institutions in Victoria and interstate as a high profile design office. Recognition has been expressed in the form of RAIA Merit Awards, invitations to participate in forums and architect in residency programs, and requests to deliver lectures to professional and academic institutions throughout Australia. Since 1984 the practice has been awarded nine awards for outstanding architecture, one commendation and has been short-listed for nine other awards, including a national RAIA Merit Award for Interior Design.

SIGNIFICANT PROJECTS

1986	Coronial Services Centre, Victoria, Australia (Contracted designer to Bates Smart & McCutcheon)	$26 million budget
1987	Melton TAFE College, Victoria, Australia (Contracted to Public Works Department)	$10 million budget
1987	Whittesea TAFE college, Victoria, Australia (Contracted to Public Works Department)	$12.6 million budget
1987	Victoria Police Accommodation Standard, Brief Development, Victoria, Australia (Contracted to Public Works Department)	
1988	Knox Police Station, Victoria, Australia (Contracted to Public Works Department)	$17 million budget
1988	Victoria Police Headquarters Feasibility Studies, Victoria, Australia (Contracted to Public Works Department)	$165 million budget
1988	Post Occupancy Evaluation, Broadmeadows Police Station, Victoria, Australia (Contracted to Public Works Department)	
1991	Municipal Offices Caulfield, Victoria, Australia (Won in a limited competition)	$5 million budget
1993–94	Armadale Cinemas, Car Park and Restaurants, Victoria, Australia	$5 million budget
1993–94	Consulting in association with architects in Singapore: Consultant design services provided on master planning of condominiums:	
	BNI Shangri La	$45 million budget
	Bukit Timah	$250 million budget
	Consultant design services provided on 350-bed resort hotel in Ganzhou, China	$75 million budget
1994–95	Tang Choon Keng Properties Pty Ltd, Singapore: Condominium development Loyang Besar Project shelved	$7 million budget
	Condominium development St Thomas Walk Project shelved	$185 million budget
1997–99	Mansaw Pty Ltd, Melbourne, Australia, designed multiple residential development in existing heritage-listed buildings including penthouse structures	$8 million budget
1999–00	Tripp Residence, Victoria, Australia Confidential budget Intrapac Pty Ltd, Victoria, Australia, commercial and residential mixed development	$7 million budget
	Lillydale and Kerang fire stations, Victoria, Australia	$1.7 million budget

EXHIBITIONS

1984   'Architecture as Idea'
        Royal Melbourne Institute of Technology Gallery, Victoria, Australia

1986   '5 AR'
        Melbourne University Gallery, Victoria, Australia

1986   'New Classicism'
        Monash University Gallery, Victoria, Australia

1990   'Take a Seat'
        Blaxland Gallery, Meyer Buidling, Victoria, Australia

1992   'Sight Regained'
        Westpac Gallery, Victorian Arts Centre, Victoria, Australia

1992   'Fin De Siècle & the 21st Century'
        Tollarno Gallery, Victoria, Australia

1993   'Whole New World'
        Panorama Gallery, Victoria, Australia

1993   'Sight Regained'
        Ivan Dougherty Gallery, University of New South Wales, New South Wales, Australia

1993   'The Perceptual Edge'
        Perth Institute of Contemporary Arts, Western Australia, Australia

1994   'Furniture 95'
        Installation for Artists in Industry, 333 Collins Street, Melbourne, Australia

1996   'Out of The Shadows', Aspects of Antipodean Architecture
        Royal Institute of Architects, Scotland Gallery, Edinburgh, Scotland

1997   '1st, 2nd & 3rd Generation Architects'
        Melbourne University Architecture Gallery, Victoria, Australia

AUSTRALIAN MERIT AWARDS

1984	Merricks Music Room, Merricks, Victoria	RAIA* Award
1985	Wurruk Primary School, Wurruk, Victoria	RAIA Finalist
1986	Warehouse Conversion, Fitzroy, Victoria (Commercial/Residential)	RAIA Finalist
1987	Rijavec Architects' Office, Fitzroy, Victoria	RAIA Award
1989	Architect's Residence, Clifton Hill, Victoria	RAIA Finalist
1989	David Ellis Fine Art Gallery, Fitzroy, Victoria	RAIA Award
1990	Lara Warehouse, Fitzroy, Victoria (Commercial/Residential)	RAIA Award
1991	Foard Freehold, Windsor, Victoria (Commercial/Studio Conversion)	RAIA Award
1991	Caulfield Town Hall, Caulfield, Victoria	RAIA Award
1992	Hooper Construction's Warehouse, Carlton, Victoria (Commercial/Studio)	RAIA Finalist
1993	Panorama Gallery and Electronic Projection Cinema, Fitzroy, Victoria	RAIA Award
1994	Francis Residence, Warrandyte, Victoria	RAIA Unbuilt Commendation
1994	Fitzroy Swimming Pool, Fitzroy, Victoria (Institutional Category)	RAIA Finalist
1994	Freeland Residence, Fitzroy, Victoria (Interiors Category)	RAIA Finalist
1994	Freeland Residence, Fitzroy, Victoria (Master Builders' Association of Victoria House of the Year)	RAIA Award
1995	Freeland Residence, Fitzroy, Victoria	RAIA Award
1997	Alessio Residence, Templestowe, Victoria	RAIA Finalist
1997	Penthouse, 357 Little Bourke Street, Melbourne	RAIA Finalist
1998	Seppelt Contemporary Art Award, Museum of Contemporary Art, New South Wales	Nomination
2000	Alessio Residence, Templestowe, Victoria (Dulux Interior Category)	Award

*RAIA: Royal Australian Institute of Architects

DESIGN PUBLICATIONS

ARTICLES

Alessi, A. 'Muro Magico'. *Costtruire* (No. 201, February 2000), pp. 123-125.

Brown, P. B. 'Chen House'. *Monument* (No. 23, 1998), pp. 68-73.

Day, N. 'Ovular Order'. *Architecture Australia* (September/October 1994), pp. 30-37.

Day, N. 'Unbuilt Promises'. *Architectural Review Australia* (No. 70, Summer 1999).

Ypma, H. 'A Great Space'. *Interior Design* (Issue 8, 1987), pp.104-110.

Dokulil, H. 'Visceral Geometry'. *Monument* (No. 5, 1995), pp. 58-61.

Dunworth, M. 'People in Glass Houses'. *Vogue Living* (September 1990), pp. 74-79.

Evans, D. *Aardvark* (Royal Melbourne Institute of Technology, Melbourne Architectural Guide) (1990-99).

Friis-Clark, A. 'The Ovoidal Atrium'. *Corporate & Office Design* (October 1991), pp. 90-93.

Jackson, D. 'Francis Residence'. *Architecture Australia* (January/February 1994), pp. 30.

Jackson, D. 'Sinuous Spaces'. *Vogue Living* (August/September 1994), pp. 124-131.

Jackson, D. 'Type Setting', *Architecture Australia* (July/August 1995), pp. 42-45.

Jurgans, Z. 'Playing With Perception'. *Belle* (No. 96, December/January 1990), pp. 58-65.

Jurgens, Z. 'Hip Baths: Fitzroy Swimming Pool'. *Corporate & Office Design* (August 1993), pp. 88-91.

Jurgens, Z. 'Industrial Revolution'. *Belle* (November 1991), pp. 154-157.

Lyon, H. 'Still Life'. *Interior Design*. (Issue 20, 1991), pp. 122-131.

Missingham, G. 'Ivan Rijavec' (Coronial Services Centre and Whittlesea TAFE College). *Transition* (Issues 18 & 19, September 1986), pp. 33-34.

Pickering, Carl. 'Traittoie Curve'. *Cassa Vogue Gennaio* (No. 181, 1987), pp. 111-115.

Rijavec, I. 'Liberty'. *Monument* (Millenium Issue, December 1999), pp. 44-47.

Rijavec, I. 'Urban Aeronautics'. *Monument* (No. 17, 1997), pp. 48-51.

Rijavec, I. 'Viewing Room'. *Transition* (Vol. 5, No. 1, June 1986), pp. 12-13.

Rijavec, I. 'Working on the Perceptual Edge'. *Fin De Siècle, Architectures of Melbourne* (1992), pp. 172-190.

Rijavec, I. 'Wurruk Primary School'. *Architecture Australia* (November 1985), pp. 54-57.

Scalzo, S. & Di Muccio, E. '90s Antics, or Whipping it Up For The Twenty First Century'. *Transition* (Issue 46, 1994), pp. 48-51.

Selenitsch, A. 'Plaster Cast'. *Interior Design* (Issue 16, 1989), pp. 100-105.

Standfield, N. 'Hooper Construction's Offices'. *Corporate & Office Design* (August 1991), pp. 75-93.

Stewart, K. 'Thinking Outside the Square'. *Houses* (Issue 20, 2000), pp. 44-47.

Van Schaik, L. 'Altered Perception'. *Inside* (No. 6, 1998), pp. 78-82.

Zellner, P. 'Warp'. *Architecture Australia* (July/August 1997), pp. 34-39.

BOOKS

Architects of the New Millennium. Melbourne: The Images Publishing Group, 2000.

Goad, Phillip. *Melbourne Architecture*. Melbourne: Watermark Press,1999.

Hubay, Tibor. *Australian Interior Design Manual*. Sydney: Allen & Unwin, 1989.

Jackson, Davina & Johnson, Chris. *Australian Architecture Now*. London: Thames & Hudson, 2000.

Michell, Jon & Gollings, John. *New Australian Style*. London: Thames & Hudson, 1999.

Pedden, Anne & Luscombe, Desley. *Picturing Architecture*. Sydney: Craftsman House,1992.

PHOTOGRAPHY CREDITS